YOU ARE HIRED! HOW TO PREPARE FOR AN INTERVIEW AND ANSWER ALL QUESTIONS

By Steve M. Carter

www.meryko-p.com

All rights reserved. No part of this publication may be reproduced, distributed, or transmitted in any form or by any means, including photocopying, recording, or other electronic or mechanical methods, without the prior written permission of the publisher, except in the case of brief quotations embodied in critical reviews and certain other noncommercial uses permitted by copyright law. For permission requests, write to the publisher, addressed "Attention: Permissions Coordinator," at the address below.

Disclaimer and Terms of Use: Effort has been made to ensure that the information in this book is accurate and complete, however, the author and the publisher do not warrant the accuracy of the information, text and graphics contained within the book due to the rapidly changing nature of science, research, known and unknown facts and internet. The Author and the publisher do not hold any responsibility for errors, omissions or contrary interpretation of the subject matter herein. This book is presented solely for motivational and informational purposes only.

Info@meryko-p.com

Copyright © 2016 by Steve M. Carter

Table of Content

Introduction 5
Understanding Your Target for job 7
Self assessment 15
Your knowledge about the company 16
Types of interview 19
    1. Behavioral interview 19
    2. Interviews based on the defining of competences or "focused" interview. 21
    3. The commission interview 21
    4. Biographical interview 22
    5. Critical interview 22
    6. Structured interview 23
    7. Unstructured interviews 23
    8. Stress interview 24
    9. Group interview 26
    10. Technical interview 28
The appearance at the interview 30
Self-presentation at the interview 33
Behavior at interview 36
Frequently asked interview questions 38
Questions with a hidden meaning at the interview 45
How to talk about your advantages and disadvantages at the interview 51

How to answer personal questions during the interview?......54
Five questions that you should definitely ask at the interview 59
First day at a new job 65
CONCLUSION 68

Introduction

The interview is the main method of evaluation and selection of candidates for employment. Interview with the employer causes stress even in professional and experienced candidates, so it is important to think in advance how to behave at a job interview, how to answer the questions asked during the interview.

It is obvious that the effectiveness of communication in the course of the interview is increased to take into account the requirements for the carrier in the aspect of general culture of speech and culture of everyday speech, in the aspect of his intellectual emotional and volitional, ethical willingness to communicate with someone.

Since in the essence any employment interview is reduced to the primary (rod, basic) questions and the corresponding answers to them, I will consider the basic questions that are asked always and without fail, and I will try to present you the best tactics of answering them. You need to have ready answers for these questions in advance. For example: Tell us a little about yourself? What attracts you to work with us in this position? What is your advantage over other candidates? etc.

The best way to avoid mistakes is to prepare well for the interview and know what mistakes are possible in general.

One false step can cost you the job! You have done so much to get to this interview. And now there is a time to come face to face with the employer. Any little thing can be decisive, everything should be under your control.

Understanding Your Target for job

You should be aware of and understand your life and career goals and see the ways to achieve them. Motivation to achieve requires also the presence of the potential for development, the life of will and energy, what are called "drive". This quality within the company transforms into a clear understanding of the goal set and aspiration of employee to achieve it, not just to the formal implementation of the list of specified work. Especially brightly this quality manifests itself in a situation where circumstances change rapidly and to achieve the goal you need to do very different steps, not those that were originally planned. Here, the ability to respond quickly to change and to achieve this goal in the new environment is important.

A person with such a quality, seeks not just to "work job", so there are no claims - he enjoys a well executed work and achievement of results.

Often, companies are looking for just such an employee - from the staff in the hotels, who knows how to properly act in unusual situations, to the heads of departments and managers of higher level.

Also, today, successful person is the one who has the right information at the right time. The volume of information and knowledge needed to achieve the set goals, grows very quickly. For this reason, the desire and the ability of employees to learn and develop are so important for companies. Teachers in universities knowingly repeat – "we will not be able to teach you everything you need for your future career, but here you can learn how and where to find information and how to quickly learn it". When you get into your first company (and in the second, third, and so on), your first task will be to study and understand in a short time a huge amount of information about products, work specifics, clients, business processes and technology of work. This is where it's time to use what you have learned in the university. To become a successful employee, you will need not only to cope with this task, but also constantly learn within the company. Career growth in any organization is directly related to the mastery of new knowledge, skills and personal development and the best employers provide their employees with many opportunities and support in development. But do not forget that the initiative in acquiring new knowledge and skills must come from you.

Passage of the interview (as well as the very career) is successful in the case where a person not knows in advance what he wants, but also what he needs it for, what he will do after achieving goals.

It is necessary to be familiar with the world of the professions and the requirements that are applied to a person who performs a particular job, to clarify for yourself a "formula" of chosen profession.

It is necessary to properly identify your interests and inclinations, to assess your potential, health status, and the ability to meet the requirements of chosen profession.

It is necessary to proceed from the real opportunities for education, retraining and advanced training.

Until recently, it was usual practice simply to indicate in resume the name of the position you are applying for. However, in today's business world, it is not enough to specify a job title. Employers want to know about a candidate much more: What motivates a candidate? Why does he want to work namely in our company? Does he know the specifics of the business? Does he understand what the company can offer him as a career and professional prospects? These are the main questions asked by the employer in the selection of candidates. Partly these questions can be answered in the line "CV objective" in CV, but you should be prepared to give a clear answer to this question in the interview.

Candidates to fill vacancies may be asked:
• about professional goal,
• about personal goal in the work
• about the purpose of professional activities,
• about the goals in life (life goals).

There are fundamental differences among these goals.

Professional goal is the result of the work of a specialist, which he gives to others (his clients or customers). Professional goal speaks of your work content and answers to the following questions: What exactly do you do? What problems you help to solve? In what way you are doing it? What exactly people will get when they turn to you for professional help? Telling the employer about your professional goals, it is not recommended to speak anything other than this.

Personal goals in the work is a result that an expert himself gets, thanks to the performance of his professional duties. This may be a personal remuneration, compensation, personal or professional prospects for growth and development of knowledge, skills, capabilities, etc. What do you expect to receive as a result of your work? The answer to this question is actually a description of your personal goals at work. Most interestingly, such a result can be either developed by the expert during the execution of the work (for example, the acquisition of certain personal and professional skills), or transferred to him by the others as compensation or remuneration for work performed (e.g., wages, state premium, opportunity to learn at the expense of the organization, or to take a more responsible working place). So everything that the expert expects to receive from others in compensation, reward, gratitude for his work, in a different way is called the expectation from work. For example, getting a job, you can expect a certain amount of wages that will be accrued to you by the employer. If you provide your income by yourself, and not with the help of the employer, then you are rather an individual entrepreneur.

Objectives of professional activity are is the results you get in the process, and either pass to others or take by yourself. Objectives of professional activity is a general term that reflects any results related to your work. That is, these goals can reflect both your personal expectations and professional goals – even together, though separate, even in the formulation of the net (only a professional or just a personal goal), even in the combined formulation (objective, incorporating elements of both professional and personal goals in the work). This may be one goal, or maybe a list of goals. But they must be relevant to your work. And here is an interesting nuance.

Questions about the purpose of work, job search, employment purposes, and the like, are questions about the same - about the purpose of your professional activity. The formulation varies depending on the circumstances in which the question is asked. For example, if you are looking for work, you may be asked about the purpose for which you do it. For what purpose do you search for jobs? .. If you have entered into a dialogue about the potential employment, you may be asked about the purpose of employment. For what purpose did you decide to find a job? .. If you work, you may be asked about the purpose of your work. What is the goal you are pursuing, efficiently performing your professional duties? .. If you managed to find the right job, then the job search objective, the purpose of the work and professional activity are almost identical. No wonder - it is one and the same goal, just in different aspects.

Among other things, questions like: "Why are you interested in this position" or "Why do you want to work in our organization?" - also fall into the category of issues tightly related to your goals of professional activity. Why are you interested namely in this position, what exactly you like about it? If you are attracted by the possibility to perform certain functions, to help certain people in addressing specific problems in specific ways, most likely, this position it allows you to realize your professional goal. Is not it? If you are tempted by wages, opportunity to gain specific professional experience, the prospect of working in a large, stable, "cool" organization, etc., then this vacancy meets your expectations from work or allows realizing personal goals that you plan to achieve by yourself. And if you are really hoping to get this particular job because you can also to deal with favorite thing to do, and get a decent salary, so this vacancy simultaneously reflects your professional and personal interest, that is, it corresponds to the combined goals of your professional activity. You see, if you formulate the goals of your professional activities in the right manner, you can easily and naturally answer almost any question related not only with the objectives but with the expectations, intentions, interests in the work. The only thing they do not touch, it is your goals, interests, intentions and plans that are not directly related to work.

Goals in life, or life goals is the result which you plan to achieve in the near or distant future, in life in general. These goals can be directly or indirectly related to your professional activity, and may be not associated with it. All the goals in life that are not related to your work, are called your private purposes. This, for example, the goals that relate to your family, children, friends, home, property, travel, hobbies, health, in the end. But here there are some nuances that are worth to know.

On the one hand, the question about life's purpose is much more democratic than the question about professional aims or personal expectations. You understand that life goals relate to absolutely all areas of your life - private, personal, professional. On the other hand, precisely because of its "total democratism", such a question can be very tough. However, no guarantee of trick or secret intent can be given here. So I will just list the main reasons why such a question is asked.

The question of life goals is asked often to:

• save time on the question of the individual aims, because in the answer it becomes clear, what exactly and in what kind of field you intend to pursue;

• understand exactly what (private, personal, professional) interests you put at the forefront, as well the things you do not really care;

• find out if you plan in the near future significant changes in life that can affect the quality or duration of your work in the company;

• test the scope of your identity, track correlation, consistency and adequacy of the objectives pursued.

Answering about the purpose of life, you can tell about the professional and personal intentions at work. If this information is not enough, the interlocutor will have to ask you a direct question. Accordingly, it will be easier to figure out what exactly organization representative is afraid of and answer so to calm his fears.

Every professional should have a clear career (or professional) aim to constantly develop and strive for more - to raise the bar. This is the most important sign of a professional which has to be traced in the description of the goal.

Self assessment

Before you go for an interview for the position you are applying for, it is very important to soberly assess your strength and find out in what you are more preferable, and what are your advantages compared with other candidates. Self assessment is the best way to approach critically to own skills, abilities, strengths and weaknesses, as well as to issues of work ethic. Self-assessment will highlight the most important, to determine what role is best suited to you and will be the basis of your future career. Critical self-evaluation period prior to the interview, will allow you to objectively evaluate your progress, advantages and success, and to identify the aspects of particular value in the work that you can get. Make a list of your motivators, your expectations from work and decide for yourself what place the work occupies in your life. This should be the basis of your conversation and determine the list of discussion questions prior to the interview.

Your knowledge about the company

It is impossible to overestimate the benefits of analyzing information about the company, which invited you for an interview. Analysis of problems, objectives and goals of the company will not only allow you to express yourself as a candidate who tends to understand the specifics of the company, but also allow you to tailor your professional knowledge, skills and experience to the unique requirements of the company.

Learn as much as possible about the organization, where you're going for an interview and about the work ahead, namely:

- What products or services the company offers?
- Where and to whom the products are sold?
- How many years the company exists?
- How much its main objectives have changed since its foundation?
- Is there enough stable leadership structure or bosses often change?
- Is the organization public or private property?
- Are the services of the organization or its products seasonal? Are the conditions of employment also seasonal?
- Was there staff reductions in the last three years? Why?

- Whether the organization is included in some larger association?

- How much attention it is paid in media? Why? What is the rating: positive or negative?

- Is the organization characterized by a conservative attitude towards employees?

- What new projects are developed there? Whether it is based only in the country or has foreign branches and links with foreign countries?

- Whether the organization belongs to a growing industry?

- What prospects exist in the industry?

Ways of getting useful information:

- Leaflets and brochures enterprises;

- Information in the media;

- Ads and other information in the office of the company;

- Employees of the organization (you can learn a lot of useful things, but it is necessary to take into account the subjectivity of "painting" of such stories).

If your analysis shows that the company which invited you for an interview is proud of its ideological leadership, make it clear in the interview that you also appreciate the ideological leadership. When preparing for an interview reflect in your CV examples of ideological leadership in your life and work. In conducting this analysis, try to get the same information about competitors.

The candidate well informed about the state of affairs in the company, will always stand out from others and stands out against the background of the ordinary job applicants that pass the interview.

Not knowing information about the company is one of the main mistakes of candidates at interviews. It shows disinterest and passivity of the candidate.

Moreover, going to the interview being so unprepared is in fact a bad taste.

You not only should to ask what the company does, but with your responses and questions you need to demonstrate that you know quite a lot about the company and came to the interview absolutely consciously, and namely in this company you want to work.

Types of interview

There are many different types of interviews, some of which have already been described above. Interview form will depend not only on the style selected by your interviewer, but also on the type of company, the position for which you apply, your personal skills and qualities of your interviewer.

After reviewing the main types and techniques of the interview, you can prepare answers to common questions and think over your behavior in the possible situations. By following these tips, you may well prove yourself, regardless of the type of interview.

Most often, the interview sare:

1. Behavioral interview

Behavioral interviewing is based on the idea that the past experience is the best indicator of future behavior in similar situations.

The employer is developing description of a job or qualifications and skills of the sought specialist. They define competence and prescribe the required level of training for the position. In advance, a list of questions is drawn up to determine the details of your behavior in the past (in the circumstances with which you are likely to encounter in the new work place), and to clarify the possession of key skills. Most likely, all the candidates will be asked the same questions. But after this interview it often seems that you were not given the opportunity to fully express your interest in this work.

To show yourself well in behavioral interviews, prepare specific examples of situations that are likely to be discussed and you will not have to think long about them during the interview. Think about possible questions and answers in advance, you can also maximize the positive impression, to strengthen interest to the work and develop a strategy for the responses to the unexpected "difficult" questions that you may encounter.

Standard questions at behavioral interview can be the following:

"Give an example of a situation where you had to choose between two important tasks with the critical deadline. How did you decide what to do? What was the result?"
and "Have you ever had to deal with very demanding, angry customers, when it is not possible to seek help from a qualified specialist in this field? What have you done? Why have you made this decision?"

For more precise suggestion about what questions you may be asked, learn the requirements of the vacant positions, the criteria for the required work experience, job description and analyze the core competencies. Think about your past experience that would demonstrate your skills in the relevant areas.

2. Interviews based on the defining of competences or "focused" interview.

This interview sets priorities on key requirements and defines the preparation of the candidate to work in the vacant position. As with behavioral interview, you will have to answer detailed questions on the identification of past experience, which is necessary to clarify the experience and attitude of the candidate for future responsibilities.

3. The commission interview

Many organizations prefer to conduct the interview with the candidate in the form of commissions, especially for large-scale attraction of new employees, such as the annual selection of young graduates. "Commission" interview is used by employers because it can accelerate the selection process, allowing all members of the commission (the interviewers) to evaluate applicants simultaneously. In addition, at this interview equal, objective assessment of all the members of the commission prevail rather than the subjective opinion of the interviewer.

In the commission interview, two to six interviewers take part. This makes the situation more formal and can be somewhat confusing for a candidate. Interviewers either alternately ask you questions, each of his fields, or mostly the conversation is conducted by a few people, while the rest take notes.

Stay confident, do not panic, try to maintain eye contact and talk to everybody at the same time. Try to look at each of those present during the interview. Focus on questions that are asked and your responses to these questions.

4. Biographical interview

In the biographical interview, the interviewer meets with your CV and talk to you about your biography, beginning with education and work experience, discussing every job in chronological order. Biographical interview is a good opportunity to show the breadth of your abilities, skills and knowledge to show personality. However, it can also detect the failure to identify the skills and experience that are most important and relevant to the position being discussed. It is very important to identify this information.

5. Critical interview

When choosing this type of interview, the interviewer focuses on conflict and turning points in your life and career, which became the strength test for you. He can talk about your studying at the University, beginning working life, the difficult aspects of your last job.

Try to make your responses respective to desired position, speak with confidence. For example, if the interviewer asks you about the reasons for dismissal, give a brief description of the circumstances, and then tell about what you learned from this experience: for example, that it helped you to re-evaluate plans for career advancement, becoming more selective in the choice of directions of development of your skills.

6. Structured interview

Some interviewers may discuss your work experience first, then motivation, personality and character. This type of interview is regulated by the interviewer. However, a clear understanding of the qualities that the employer considers to be important can help you to focus on the skills and experience necessary for the discussed position.

7. Unstructured interviews

Some employers use a simpler method of interview, relying on you in conducting of the main part of the conversation. Typically, such an interview begins with the words: "Tell me about yourself" and then interviewer turns to the moment of your biography, which are of the most interest for him. This type of interview is used to test your ability to self presentation or because the interviewer does not want, cannot or does not see the need to conduct the conversation on this stage in more structured way.

This interview can appear to be difficult if you are shy or unprepared, but it gives a good opportunity to focus on the strengths and your skills and experience necessary for this position.

8. Stress interview

Stress interview is conversation, during which the employer creates tension or conflict situation, criticizing and questioning the statements of candidates, as well as frequently asking unclear, unethical or difficult or even unacceptable questions. The purpose of this interview is to assess your behavior in stressful situations. Stress interview is mainly used for the selection of candidates for the position with a high degree of tension. This unpleasant interview is the difficult test and is not used for the majority of positions. In addition, it requires special skills from the interviewer.

Most job seekers will not face a stressful interview during the job search. However, it is important to have an idea of how to behave in such a situation and how to answer unexpected questions. Sometimes a short, but pleasant and professional refusal to respond to a question or request for clarification of pertinence of question may be precisely the reaction that the employer expects from you.

Cases of outright rudeness, psychological oppression, as well as other actions assaulting dignity are extremely rare. On the part of the employer, demonstration of aggression is extremely ill-considered strategy of behavior: such an approach only candidates who have nothing to lose will remain, because they are not hired anywhere else. Adequate and competitive professionals unlikely will meet such ""creativity" with understanding, even in times of crisis.

More often, applicants have to deal with stress interview in the style of "tough negotiations". Usually, there is a certain tough stage, after which the interview goes into the business mainstream.

The tension stage is usually included to interviews with top managers, experts in working with clients and claims, sales managers, secretaries and personal assistants, staff of call centers and some of the other candidates.

At this, different cases, "attacks", hard or strange questions, manipulations are applied. All these actions are accompanied by the appropriate intonation.

Examples of "non-standard" questions of the recruiter, in communication of which job applicant' response to objections and criticism is estimated: "I'm sorry, but I did not understand anything!" Or "It looks like you were not doing a lot in this field?".

Or it can be, for example, question –case from HR: "Imagine that you are lost in the woods without food or water. Your actions?"

Occasionally, interviewers use role-playing techniques according to the "good and bad investigator" and the like.

Open attacks emotional or role techniques usually are easily recognized.

More subtle ways of influencing can be determined, if for a moment to listen to your feelings: you suddenly feel unusual emotions appeared, which you did not expect, for example, the dudgeon. Or the emotion itself can be expected, but its strength exceeds the usual threshold.

If you notice something "wrong", it is important to preserve the dignity and peace of mind. In response to uncomfortable and even unethical questions it is undesirable:
- To ignore the question,
- To bustle, make excuses,
- To show dissatisfaction and argue,
- To go to the conflict.

Of course, there is always the opportunity to just get up and leave. But it should be understood that the stress interview is an emotional game, and nothing more. And this game can and should be played correctly. Remember that "stress" questions - these are questions away the point. This is not an insult, but "testing" your identity.

It should be understood that the stress-stage of the dialogue is not related to how your skills and experience correspond to the vacant position for which you are applying. It relates to the qualities of your personality.

9. Group interview

In case of using this kind of interview, applicants are asked to perform together some task or discuss in the group with the interviewer a specific topic. As a rule, such an interview is used by large companies in the selection of a large number of specialists. This interview usually has two aims: to consider a large number of candidates in a short time, considering their different qualities (ease of communication, management skills and approach to solving the problem), and determine the suitability of candidates for the company's goals, their ability to work in a team.

Each representative of the company participating in a job interview has his own list of questions that you must answer, as well as his own set of criteria for evaluating your competence. There are good reasons for the participation of each company representative in a job interview, and due to this it is important to show the same attitude to each of them; do not be tempted to communicate only with your potential supervisor. If the interview with you is conducted by a group of representatives of the company, you must maintain eye contact with each of them. Try to keep your answer to the next question one way or another been associated with the problem, previously set by another representative of the company. Such an approach will create an atmosphere of harmonious interaction between all members of the group and will allow you to show that you understand the role and importance of each participant.

Before you come to the interview, try to determine the position and function of each participant of group of interviewers. For example, if you are to be interviewed at the same time with the manager on work with clients, chief financial officer and the head of the personnel department, it is rational to be familiar with current information about the company customers policy, financial and personnel policies. Be prepared to ask questions relating to the competence of each member of interviewers group. This will allow you to show how well you can communicate with different departments of the organization.

Group interviews are usually conducted with the participation of several candidates applying for one position. The purpose of this type of interview is to find out how candidates interact with each other.

Some group interviews are part of the game scenarios of real situations simulation, according to which you are entrusted to any task relevant to the position for which you are applying. The goal of the task is to find out how you will cope with your responsibilities. Each candidate is evaluated by how well he copes with functions that may be assigned to him in real life. It allows employers to more accurately identify the most suitable candidates, comparing them with each other.

If you participate in a group interview, it is important to be perceived as an active participant, not just an observer. Suggest your ideas and opinions, but do not forget to listen carefully to the other candidates. Resist the temptation to dominate in the conversation and interrupting other participants even if you want to.

10. Technical interview

Technical interviews are different in that they ask questions about the position to which you are applying. Based on your answers, the interviewer determines how well you can cope with the technical problems associated with the post. Despite the importance of the demonstration of technical knowledge in the interview, it should be noted that your interviewer is not so much interested in it as in your approach to problem solving, how you analyze these problems and what personal qualities you possess. Technical interviews are necessary in order to demonstrate the recruitment staff your knowledge and skills to solve problems associated with the new position to which you are applying. Therefore, for some of them it will be more interesting to evaluate your level of technical knowledge required, for example, for software development; others will pay attention to your approach to solving problems related to technical aspects of the new job.

The appearance at the interview

It would seem, a neat suit and clean shoes must be evident dress code for an interview, but as practice shows, not all job seekers think what they will put on a meeting with a potential employer. The appearance at the interview is no less important than punctuality.

Complete disregard for style is a big mistake. Many people believe that they should be evaluated for what they are, but this is not often the case. Some employers are willing to hire such a candidate, but it is a very rare case, and the candidate must be a genius. The rest should take into account the basic laws of social influence, it will help to win over a potential employer.

Appearance is not only a manifestation of own identity, but sign of respect of human to himself and to the partner in conversation. This would mean that the applicant perceives himself holistically, paying attention not only to the professional development, but also the appearance, which speaks of his attitude and social status. Interview is a formal meeting, so neat or business style is most acceptable, and can be a criterion for selection.

Accessories - handbags, watches, pen - also can tell much of the job seeker. Particular care in their selection should be shown by applicants for managerial positions: it is important to find a middle ground between the presentability and excessive luxury. At the same time, employers are unanimous: the lack of accessories is much better than their overabundance. Piercing of the face and bright beads in several rows hardly help career.

According to 18% of human resources professionals, the main in the competitor' appearance is neatness and tidiness. "Sloppy appearance pushes the most"; "Better is inexpensive but neat suit than expensive than unkempt one"; "Neatly. Ripped jeans, a deep neckline, peeling nail polish are unacceptable,"- these are usual HR comments. Rules are banal, but always in fashion: clothing and footwear should be clean. In any case, grab a brush and a sponge for clothes for shoes to be able to freshen up before the interview. Do not overdo with smell: no matter how trendy the spirits are, their fragrance may not be liked by your interlocutor.

Dress "in accordance with the post, applied for by the candidate" is recommended by 11% of HRs, another 7% advise to ask in advance the requirements of the employer company to the appearance of employees. "It depends on the position. For specialists casual style is better. Managers should always prefer official style; It is better to pre-acquainted with the dress code of the company", - employers say.

Indeed, in some cases, a business suit and tie may not be appropriate - for example, if you are a designer and came to the interview in an advertising agency. Journalists, photographers and PR specialists can dress in more free style. Your appearance at the interview must call in others the impression that you are their soul mate and share their tastes. Do not look like a black sheep - dress appropriately to the environment, i.e. as the other office staff dresses up.

It is rational to conduct a little reconnaissance before the interview. Explore not only the company's history, its successes and the current plans, but also corporate traditions, which include the dress code. Try to look like an ordinary employee of the company. Then the employer unwittingly introduce the candidate to the role of his employees, it will be easier to associate the competitor with the current team.

The appearance of the candidate must comply with the direction of the company activity. If you go for an interview at the bank, it is unlikely that the free form of clothing will cause the good attitude in the employer. In this case, a restrained and conservative style of dress is more suitable.

Designers, journalists, advertisers, and other representatives of creative professions is not the case. A classic suit and tight tie is not the best solution for them. On the contrary, welcomed liberties in the wardrobe will be welcomed, which emphasize the individuality and creativity inherent and necessary in this profession.

Self-presentation at the interview

Self-presentation is a kind of demonstration of yourself to the employer as part of his team. For effective representation you need to demonstrate your ability to integrate into the team, your professional skills, corporate appearance, corresponding to the company activity and the desired position, and show your preparation for the interview.

Pre-employment interview may be accompanied by nervous tension. To make a good impression, you should spend some time on a neat appearance, gestures and overall behavior. If you look respectively, demonstrate the experience and skills required for the job, then you have done everything you could to obtain the desired position.

Making a good impression at the interview is difficult without a thorough home preparation. Sit down and think about how and what you will be talking to a potential employer, arm with facts confirming your achievements in previous jobs, think over the answers to all possible questions. Such psychological training will allow you to feel more confident in the interview, to conduct a dialogue on an equal footing, ad just lift your spirits.

Typically, as it was stressed above, during the interview the employer asks the candidate to tell about himself. It is important not to get lost and to highlight the main thing that characterizes you - as a person and as a professional. Tell about how you realize yourself in the chosen profession, what have achieved over the years, and what you want to achieve on the position that interests you in the new company. Speak quickly, clearly and convincingly, without "water" and the lyrical digressions - only the most important, directly related to the purpose of your visit – to get a desired job.

At the interview you should not only interest employer with your persona, but also show a return of interest to the company, a job in which you want to receive. When the organization was founded, how the business processes of the department in which you are want to work are arranged, what is expected from you in the very first months of work and what career opportunities may open up later? Such interest is an additional plus in your favor.

Self-presentation - it's what creates your image, even when you are not next to the person. The telephone conversation or an e-mail - it is also a way to express yourself. The next day after a meeting with recruiter it is useful to call or send a letter in which you give thanks for the meeting and attention given to you and interest politely when the decision on your candidature will be made. Such a conversation or a letter is not only an element of business etiquette. It can help you in time to correct the mistake made during interview, or to clarify the details.

It is believed that humans have only 30 seconds to hit fancy. This rule is effective also in employment. Your task is to make sure that after your appearance a recruiter wants to talk more and more with you. Making a positive first impression will be contributed by elaborated appearance for a visit to a potential employer. Your voice is also an important touch to the portrait, so try to sound confident, but at the same time politely. And, of course, be punctual - serious professionals (and in fact you are just such) are not late to business meetings!

Behavior at interview

In order not to be late for an interview, be sure to find out where the company is located, how to travel, how much time will be spent on the road. Come to the interview is best little earlier, but did not seek to get ahead. It is better to just stay in the office of the company, look at the way it looks, and what happen in it, i.e., to adapt to the environment.

Arriving at the office, try to be polite and patient with all. Conscientiously fill in all questionnaires and forms that you will be offered.

Turn off the cell phone before the interview, so that nobody will disturb you (the more other employers). Otherwise it will be not only a mistake, but manifestation of disrespect.

Upon entering the cabinet of the employer, remember that 90% of opinion about you is formed in the first 90 seconds of meeting and that it will not be possible to impress once again the same people. So stay away from the employer's social communication area.

Stand straight, but relaxed. If you are constantly worried about what to do with your hands and feet, you "radiate" a sense of inconvenience and loss of self-control. Beautiful expressive posture shows the inherent dignity of the person.

Be sure to observe your behavior, no matter how professional you are. Few like to communicate with arrogant people, and HRs are not an exception - every day they are faced with dozens of competitors, of which not all have good manners. You need to bring your gestures to automatism showing friendliness and openness: the palm turned upwards, no "lock" of the arms and legs and artificial barriers in the form of a handbag or a pen in front of you and a recruiter.

Stay with dignity, be careful not to give the impression of a failure or suffering human; but refrain from provoking behavior manners.

Do not think about the answer for long, but do not hurry. Make sure that your answers to the questions were moderate and correct - without unnecessary gestures.

Frequently asked interview questions

Tell us about yourself?

This question can be asked to assess your personality, preparedness, communication skills and ability to "think on the fly". Prepare a list of what you do (your present or last job), your strengths (in relation to your work), and a brief tour of the path of your career, tying your experience to the desired job.

Why do you have left your last job?

Respond positively: ".. for better career development or a possible promotion, more responsibility, more diversity in work .."

Why do you want to do this job / work for our company?

Show off your knowledge of the company and emphasize your compliance with this position.

What can you offer us?

This is a chance to chat to talk about how cool you are concentrating on your existing skills required for this position.

For example: "I am a good seller, good team worker and really want to work in the new markets that you develop in this region". Do not forget to reinforce your skills and abilities by the examples.

What do you think this position involves?

This question is to find out whether or not you thought deeply about this post, did some studies relating to the company, and if you can summarize this information clearly.

What do you know about our company?

Demonstrate your interest in this job, your understanding / view about the organization and the industry to which it relates. Tell about your research, on the key interests of the company, its size, the main customer, current status, mentioning what sources of information you used.

Do you want to ask any questions?

Always prepare the questions you want to ask the interviewer (some of them will be considered below). Ask about the position, ask for more details to explain general information about the company, or summarize your understanding of the company, asking for confirmation, for example: "What do you see the main task for a person skilled in this position?" "Do I understand rightly that this position involves interaction between divisions A and B, monitoring and development of new approaches?"

What do you think are your strengths?

Prepare specific examples of where your strengths were demonstrated in previous work, which will help in the competition for this position.

What, in your opinion, are your weaknesses?

Nobody usually recognizes real weaknesses in competing for a new job. It is well known that it is possible to turn this question into a positive. Think about what was in your work such that it can be perceived as a weakness, but at the same time it is not perceived negativity. For example, "I pay too much attention to detail" or "I'm too fond of projects that I am involved in".

Why did you change so much jobs (companies)?

If you have changed a lot of jobs in various companies in various positions within a short period, then try to describe it positively: that you developed new skills, trying out different career paths, etc. Please refer to the past experience, which is valuable for the position.

What do you like / liked to do most on the current / last job?

The catch of the matter is that in the answer you need to highlight issues that may be related to a new place of work and show that you want to widen your experience in these areas.

Issues relating to confidential information about previous work may be checking of your prudence and professionalism. It is best to say that you would prefer not to disclose commercial information (such as sales figures, the development plans, the company's problems, etc.). A potential employer will evaluate you as a person who knows how to keep a trade secret.

What are your plans for the next 5 years?

This question helps to assess your ambition and career development plans. You must show that you are serious about further career growth and development in this sphere of activity.

Give an example of your creative abilities / management skills / organizational skills

Consider a few examples to prove that you have the key knowledge and skills described in the announcement of the vacancy and essential for this position. Most likely, these are namely the points which your interviewer will pay special attention to.

Can you work under pressure?

Responding positively, give an example of your work under pressure and describe how you coped with the difficulties, accepted the challenge.

Tell me how you do when something goes wrong? Tell us how you behave in conflict situations at work? Have you ever had to deal with the limitation of terms of performance of multiple tasks? How do you prioritize?

These questions are designed to assess your behavior in the mode of lack of time. Tell about such events at your past jobs, and always try to make a positive impression with your answer (for example, you have learned many useful things from this experience).

Learn to distinguish between:
- Irrelevant questions
- "Difficult" questions

Irrelevant questions. If you are asked a question that you think is not correct (unethical) and / or irrelevant, solve the situation with dignity. Politely ask them to explain how does it relate to the considered position. For example, "I do not understand how this issue relates to my ability to perform the work under discussion. Could you explain to me why you are interested and I will try to give relevant information".

"Difficult" questions. If you have had the experience of conflict with the employer (under- or over-spending, sexual harassment or difficulties in communicating with colleagues), get ready for what you will be asked about it in interviews for employment. It is best to answer honestly, confidently, avoiding criticism of previous employers and expressions of discontent.

For example:

"I was asked to leave the company. The official reason for that was dissatisfaction with my work ..."

... "But I do not agree with this assessment and believe that the dismissal was based on personal animosity rather than a lack of professional qualifications. If you contact with my recommendations from other companies, you will realize that I never have similar problems happened, and I'm sure that they will not occur again".

... "Unfortunately, last year I had some personal difficulties I had to overcome. I faced the choice to focus on these issues or on my work, and I chose the first. Because of it really my work suffered. Now I am again ready to devote myself to work and I am confident that I meet all your requirements".

Sexual harassment / personal encounter:

"I decided to leave because of some personal problems in the workplace, which I would prefer not to discuss".

"Due to confidentiality, I'd rather not discuss it".

Most of the applicants for an interview cannot avoid the question about the reasons for the dismissal of the previous work. It is good if you left the former company solely for the purpose of further professional growth and development - such a response will demonstrate your recruiter high internal motivation to work and be with a point in your favor. But what if the reason for dismissal was a serious conflict with management or colleagues?

It should be understood that the detailed story about how you was treated by the boss and how you suffered from minor sabotage of colleagues will be very serious drawback in the eyes of HR-manager. Such a competitor may be considered as a conflict person, unconstructive and not knowing how to work in a team.

On the other hand, an obvious deception on your part ("Relationship with the head were excellent, I just wanted to develop in the adjacent field") – this is at least unethical, and as a maximum it is dangerous for a career. After all, a lie can be revealed if the recruiter, for example, decides to ask for recommendations at your former place of work.

The best way here is to find the middle ground. Think about your answer so that it was not tricked, but not deprived you of job opportunities. Do not criticize the former chief behind back, be prepared to find something good in the resulting experience with it. "We disagreed with the former head in views on certain business issues. I understood that the company is not ready for the reforms that I propose, and decided to look for another job"; "I am grateful to the team for what it taught me to work within the frequently changing conditions, but still my goal is a bit different work" - such responses, if they sound sincere, will satisfy the recruiter.

Questions with a hidden meaning at the interview

Often, in response to the employer's questions, candidates say something that should present them in a good light. To learn about the job seeker more than he wants to say, recruiters can ask specific cunning questions.

Many of the applicants before the interview study possible questions and prepare answers to them. However, an employer can not simply ask the question directly, but make it so that the candidate does not understand his true intentions. The recruiter can also start a conversation with general topics to get your good feeling, and then use the tricky questions to find out accurate information.

HRs know that in the analysis of the candidate it is important to know the level of his self-esteem. It can serve as a starting point for predicting his future behavior on the job. But everyone believes that he estimates himself correctly. At this, special questions can give a recruiter more precise information:

• "Tell us about your successes". Candidates are more open to respond to the word "success" rather than "achievement" considering that the achievements can only be in leadership positions. Therefore, namely such a question can get you to open up. If you cannot answer this question, the employer decides that you are either too modest or cannot carry out your work at the proper level.

• "Have you ever been denied employment? If - yes, what do you think, why?". This is a very awkward question, but it allows the employer to accurately determine your self-esteem by comparing your thoughts on this issue and details of the experience and skills.

• "In what team do you feel most comfortable?" If you say that you prefer to work in a team of professionals, most likely, you are not afraid of competition, you have leadership skills and high self-esteem. Note that high self-esteem should go together with good skills and achievements. If you say that you prefer the friendly staff, then the teamwork is not option for you. It can also mean that for the work you need support and help of colleagues.

The reasons why a candidate changed his places of work, define much - his values, degree of proneness to conflict, etc. Direct question can be followed by a socially acceptable answer - lack of career development, for example. Therefore, the recruiter can go the other way:

• "How do you feel about the changes? What motivates you to change something in your life?" It turns out that not your weaknesses are discussed but your general principles of life. And on this subject, you can philosophize more sincerely. In this case, expect the also clarifying questions.

- "How do you think why employees change jobs?" Again, this question will withdraw you from the idea that the question is directed namely to your personality and your potential weaknesses. You answer as if about others, but starting from your own experience.

- "On what parameters did you choose the previous places of work?".Then clarifying questions will follow: "What has changed since the beginning of your work?", "What were the pros and cons?", etc. Again, focus here is not specifically on your personality, so HR can expect more truthful answers that easily characterize you.

Remember that first and foremost the employer assesses you, as if he did not. This is not the whole list of possible questions with a hidden meaning, but it will give you a general idea about the intentions and methods, which may be used by the interviewer.

As it is known, there are result-oriented and the process-oriented employees. Result orientation implies that the fruits of work can be measured both quantitatively and qualitatively. Results-orientation first of all is needed for middle managers and senior managers, PR- and HR-managers, marketers, salespeople, real estate agents and other employees whose salary depends on completed transactions. Staff focused on the process is more than inclined to perform repetitive operations. They are more motivated to stability, prefer a definite schedule.

It is believed to be result-oriented is more prestigious, although this is not always true. Therefore, to the recruiter' direct question: "What is more important to you: the work process or the result of work" the applicant will reply that the result is more important, although this may not be the case. But employers have other options:

• "Tell me how you were looking for previous work" A candidate who is more focused on the results of work, will describe the process of job search with a few highlights, and will not go into details. Candidate oriented mostly on the process will describe everything in detail: CV writing, publishing it, responses to the vacancies, passing through interviews, etc.

• "What should be your ideal vacation?" Employee focusing on results will tell where he will go, what impressions he expects, what sights he wants to see, i.e. will accurately describe the final result. A person aimed at the process will pay more attention to the description of how he wants to spend time swimming, sunbathing, spend time with the kids, etc.

• "Do you do sports?" According to the observations, the people who are actively involved in sports are more focused on results. Also, it is considered if it is a team sport or an individual.

How a candidate builds relationships to colleagues and superiors? Whether he is inclined to conflicts? It is not difficult to imagine how a competitor will answer such direct questions. But experienced recruiters know how to ask rightly:

• "Describe your former leaders". The recruiter will not ask to call the names and companies but will ask to give only general characteristics. From the responses of the candidate it will be possible to understand what type of leaders is more convenient for him to work with, what qualities the candidate values, and which not. This will help to understand whether a future employee will pull together with leadership in the new workplace.

• "What would you do to find a common language with the leadership?" This is a difficult question that will make you think. And because of the limitations of time, you most likely will answer based on past experience. The answers will help the employer to determine your personal qualities: communication skills, proneness to conflict, loyalty, etc.

• "Was the staff considered valuable on your previous jobs and how it was manifested or was not manifested?" In this question, attention is transferred from the candidate to the former companies and colleagues, which increases the likelihood of more honest answers. The candidate will answer based on personal opinion, his own principles, impressions and experiences, and this will provide valuable information.

Remember that employer may well talk with you about abstract topics, but the answers will tell a lot about you as a person. No matter how the questions are built, the employer is interested in revealing your qualities, rather than how bad was your former manager.

How to talk about your advantages and disadvantages at the interview

"Tell us about your pros and cons" - this is probably one of the most common questions in the interview. Someone is offered to name three of their weaknesses and three strengths, others are asked to describe the personality traits that hinder or help them in building a career – there are a plenty of options how recruiters formulate this question.

First, let's understand why this issue consistently ranks among the most frequently asked during the interview. What recruiters want to hear from the candidates? Honest confession of laziness and lack of organization or pompous speech of "I have virtually no weaknesses"?

Neither one nor the other. By asking the applicant about his advantages and disadvantages, a specialist of recruitment wants to know how mature is a person sitting in front of him, what is his self-esteem, if he is able to work constructively, including on himself. as it is known, there are no people without flaws: we are all woven of good and bad qualities. Namely in their recognition psychologists tend to see a sign of a stable and mature personality.

However, you do not need to invent anything to show recruiters that you fully meet the job requirements. Lying at the interview will not help you make a career. Be honest, but think over your answer in view of the given recommendations:

"I'm working on it ...". First of all, show that whatever your flaws, you are working to fix them and know how to compensate for them. Here are some examples.

"I always try to keep everything under control. In life and in the work it gives me a lot of inconvenience: people do not like that I constantly control their actions. So I'm learning to delegate, try not to ask too many questions on work progress to subordinates, even if I can not wait to see how things are going"; "When I studies in college, I was often late for classes and meetings. Now I have learned to appreciate my and others' time: I put the alarm clock on the early morning, and if there are serious jams in the city, I going to work on the subway. Now, I always come to the office for 10 minutes before the start of the working day" - such responses will quite satisfy recruiters. You show that you have an adequate self-esteem, you are able to recognize your mistakes and most importantly - to work constructively on them.

Lows in the pros. Psychologists believe that the best practice is response to a question about the shortcomings at the interview indirectly pointing out own advantages. "Friends think I'm meticulous. I really scrupulous, like checking all the details, and it annoys people. But I'm trying to learn to look at things more widely," – this is an excellent response of the applicant applying for the position of design engineer. "I think I am over-talkative, perhaps this is a consequence of my profession" - a good option for a candidate for the position of PR-manager or marketing specialist.

Another option of answer to the question about the shortcomings is to mention the lack of professional knowledge, not directly related to the desired position. Thus, you will demonstrate your recruiters frankness and willingness to develop. For example, if you are applying for a position of news feed reporter, you can safely admit that so far have not mastered the genre of the essay: in this work, you likely will not need this skill in the near future. However, you should still be careful not to harm yourself - think carefully about the answer.

Think about how the qualities which you are going to tell recruiters will create for you a competitive advantage over other candidates. For example, do not point to your leadership skills where they are not needed. "I'm pretty ambitious," - says the candidate for the post of accountant in a company with an established structure and ... left without a job offer. But in the young company, vigorously seizing market, such quality may well come in handy.

How to answer personal questions during the interview?

In preparation for the interview, many job seekers think through in advance the answers to possible questions - about the professional accomplishments, the reasons for leaving previous job, career goals. But personal questions are often taken by surprise. What recruiters want to know, asking, for example, about the reasons for divorce or the presence of chronic diseases in the child? How to respond to such questions, and whether to do it?

In most cases, questions about the private life are not caused by idle curiosity of recruiters; they have very specific goal - a more or less accurate psychological profile of the candidate. Experienced hiring managers know that often information which, at first glance, is not related to the professional qualities of the applicant, says more about him than he was talking about himself. That is why many HRs go for a violation of ethical norms and show interest to the private life of the candidate.

For the successful employment psychologists advise not to neglect the possible answers to personal questions: "What you care about that?" "Why do you want to know?" - such counter-questions to address HR management hardly will benefit your career. Try to find an opportunity to respond, and if the question seems too personal, politely and gently turn the conversation in another direction.

"Do you live with parents or separately?" - it would seem, what does this have to do with future work in the position of sales manager? Meanwhile, detailed response to this question can talk about such personal characteristics of the applicant, as the maturity, independence, responsibility towards the family, as well as on the level of his income. If a candidate talks about high earnings in the previous place of work, but he lives in a studio apartment with his parents or other relatives, recruiter may begin to doubt his sincerity, and hence the level of professionalism.

"Do you have your own apartment or rent it?" – this is another frequent question during the interview. At first glance, what interest business recruiter has to jobseekers property? Most likely, in such way the personnel manager is trying to understand the structure of your costs. It's one thing if the candidate has his own housing, the other - if he is forced to save each month rather big amount to pay the rent of apartment, and the third - if he pays the mortgage. In addition, the answer to this question will help supplement your psychological portrait of valuable information - whether you are willing to bear a serious responsibility to the credit institution.

Many young women have heard on interview questions like, "When you are planning to have a baby?" Of course, this is a very personal question, and often job applicant lost in answering it. After all, it is not always possible to accurately plan the birth of a baby: it is a question not only of the desire but also the state of health.

Desire of recruiter to know about your plans is clear: not all employers are willing to invest in the adaptation of the employee, which soon plans to leave on maternity leave. How to answer this question - directly or evasive, you decide. "In the near future we do not plan to have children" – such a response do not oblige you to anything, and thus dispels some fears of employer.

By law, you cannot be refused to be accepted for a job if you want to become a mother, or are already pregnant. However, it is likely that the true cause of refusal in this case will not be communicated.

"How often your child is sick?" is one more personal question, often asked by women during the interview. At this, for recruiter it does not matter what the temperature accompanies a cold in a baby - he is more concerned about the frequency and duration of your sick lists. It is better to answer frankly, because it is important also for you: the HR manager asks you to prioritize. If the career for you at the moment is no less important than the education of offspring, boldly answer that there is someone to look after baby. "The child is sick as often as other children, but grandmother (nurse, husband, etc...) is ready to stay with him" - this answer is quite satisfactory for the employer.

"What are you fond of?", "Do you have any hobbies?" – asking such questions recruiters are trying to figure out what are your temperament and character, whether you are suitable for the position by personal qualities. If, for example, the candidate claims to PR-manager position in a young and rapidly growing company, but says that he spends weekends in a chair knitting, the manager on staff will have reasonable doubts in his sociability.

"What is the last book you read?" – this is a question for revealing the overall development of the candidate. What he reads - only professional literature or finds the time to reread the classics? Although the objectivity of this method could be argued, it is still applied. There is no need to compose a list of literature, which, as it seems to you, makes you smarter in the eyes of a hiring manager. It is better to call the two books that you really have read recently: one professional and one fiction. Thus, you show that you develop not only as a professional but also as a person.

Personal questions are not uncommon in the interviews, and how you respond to them, to some extent, the decision about accepting you in a new team depends on. Therefore, talking with recruiters, be polite, diplomatic and sincere. If you do not want to respond to some particularly personal question - calmly and kindly tell that you are not ready to discuss it.

Five questions that you should definitely ask at the interview

The interview is in full swing, and you already talked about your education, accomplishments and explained why you would like to work in this company. What can be added to build on the success and to make the right career decision? It is important to ask the right questions about the future work. Moreover, their sequence (which question to ask first, and with what it is better not to hurry) is also important.

The first question: on the content of the work

Of course, during the interview, you probably already discussed what will be part of your responsibilities. In addition, it is usually described in the vacancy announcement. Therefore, in your question you need to clarify what remains unclear in functions.

For example, you have to get a PR-manager position in the existing Department of Public Relations. Ask what will be your role in establishing PR-communications. What is more important for the expert joining the team - to be literate and creative text writer and talented organizer?

Another example is interview for the position of sales assistant in the perfume shop. You have already discussed that you will be responsible for advising clients, work with a cash register and lay out of goods. Narrow how it is accepted to advise customers on the trading floor – to expect their questions or to provide information about the range of the store?

Questions about the functionality should be asked necessarily, even if everything seems clear and understandable: it will emphasize your high motivation and show the recruiter you are responsible and professional person.

The second question: about the tasks

Be sure to ask about the strategic objectives of your future work. What future employer expects from you, for example, in the annual term? What are the criteria for evaluating the effectiveness of your work?

For example, a contender for the position of Sales Manager may ask, what is the sales plan for the next year. A candidate for the position of Inspector of the Human Resources can ask about the intended increase in the number of staff and, consequently, the amount of work.

Thus, you show that you know how to think strategically and plan your activities. In addition, a clear understanding of your tasks in the company is the real engine of career. You will always be able to self-assess your work using performance criteria specified at interview.

The third question: how to quickly integrate into the team

Be sure to ask, what will be your first working days. Is induction training is planned? Will you have a mentor, who can be contacted on any issue? What are the criteria by which to measure the success of the probation period?

This question is particularly important if the work is something new for you. For example, if you previously worked in a small company, and now you have come to an international corporation; or if you were engaged in PR in retail, and now - in the restaurant business.

Question Four: Why this vacancy occurred?

The answer to this question may give you food for thought. If the job is new, then you will have to make a schedule of work and discuss in detail the responsibilities and strategic goals with the supervisor and HR-manager. It is necessary also to think about the means of achieving these goals - in fact a vacancy is new, and earlier this work was not carried out.

If there a position exists in the company for a long time, pay attention to the reasons for the dismissal of the previous employee. Of course, they can be very different – this employee found a more interesting job, did not cope with the responsibilities, has gone on leave for child care or was fired for unethical behavior.

Not the fact that HR-manager will tell you the correct information on such a sensitive issue, but it is worth to ask and to think. If you the position was left by five people for the year, you should look for additional information about the company, and the atmosphere in the team.

Question Five: salary, vacation, lunch.

You should not hurry with asking these questions - ask them at the end of your meeting, discussing all the duties, tasks and work plan. The main thing is to adequately assess your own value on the labor market and not to overestimate the value of the lunch break in the career. Of course, the applicant needs to find out all the conditions of future work, but this should be done very correctly. You agree that any question can be formulated differently. Therefore you should not interest in the forehead, whether there is paid sick leave - the employer may decide that you are going to take it often.

On what signs you can find out that the recruiter is not interested in you and what to do in such situations

Detachment, disinterest of recruiter is expressed primarily in the non-verbal signs: posture, plastic movements, facial expressions, gestures. He pulls back, some deviates from the negotiating table, unconsciously increasing the distance to the interlocutor, throws back his head, often looking around, distracts, takes the "closed" pose.

If the dynamics of movement of the recruiter's hand and speed of his speech are different, most likely the person is already thinking about something else, and a conversation does not take his attention much. He asks dry formal questions like, "Tell me about your responsibilities at the latest place of work", "Why did you decide to leave the company N". If the candidate is interesting for the interviewer, he will speak with him in a different manner.

Irritation, negative reaction of the recruiter to the behavior of the candidate can be identified by the nervous tapping a pen or other object on the surface of the table, a nervous turning pages, "shifty" look. The conversation may look "torn", questions are not consistent, and may contain latent aggression: "Your colleagues say that it is hard to work with your, do you think, why?" or "Is it true that your last project was not successful, and brought great losses to the company?".

The signs by which one can understand that the conversation is over, and the recruiter has already made decision, even if the conversation is formally still in progress: the interlocutor looks at his watch, at the door, distracts to messages in his phone, closes the diary and begins to clear table of the papers, sets clothes straight, his posture changes expressing a desire to get up. In a speech past tense verbs begin to flicker: "spoke", "discussed", " said" - all this indirectly means that the interviewer considers the interview ended.

Can a candidate influence such situation? Of course! If the candidate does not want to give up and decided to fight to the last, it is necessary to try to turn the tide of conversation, to take it in hand. It is possible to activate account recruiter' attention by interesting example of professional practice, colorful history, perhaps with a bit of humor. Timely asked questions, reflecting the understanding of the topic and interest in the work, will help the candidate to change the subject, to make the conversation more active and emotional.

To overcome irritation of interlocutor-recruiter, it is necessary to agree with him, to accept his point of view, at least partially, to stop competing. Emotional agreement helps turn rivalries into a constructive dialogue, and contributes to more productive dialogue.

First day at a new job

You will likely remember the first day at a new job for a long time. And it is not so important whether you first come to work or not, whether it is period of probation or permanent position. In addition to you, this day will be remembered even by your colleagues and your boss. This is indicated by all the articles on the theme of adaptation, and your personal experience surely confirms it. Most people are experiencing great stress on the first working day, which is usually not associated with real difficulties, and is caused by our fears, imagination, complexes.

Unfortunately, it is not possible to to give definitive advice on how to behave on the first working day. Like you, each company has its own individual characteristics. Maybe you're lucky - in the company your first day of work will be scheduled by the minutes by HR, you will be given your workplace, e-mail and so on; and maybe everything will be vice versa – you will be noticed only when you the third time remind about yourself to the secretary at the reception desk, a table will be allocated to you in a week, and you will receive corporate e-mail in three weeks. You must understand that neither the company name nor its dimensions guarantee anything: you can be forgotten about in a large company while in a small company HR-processes can be placed at the highest level. Anyway, your should adequately react on the situation.

Finally, the third component of your success in the first working day is a good preparation to the date of commencement. You can avoid a lot of problems, and gain extra points in the eyes of your new colleagues, if you take the time beforehand to prepare for the beginning of work.

Preparing to commencement begins at the interview, in extreme cases - at the time of the adoption of a job offer. If you have these steps behind, and you have not asked the right questions, find a pretext to call the company and, as it were at the same time, specify the missing details.

What you need to know at the interview to prepare for commencement:

1. Who will meet you the first time in the office. Whom do you contact in case of emergencies.

2. How and when will you learn about the introduction procedures of the company (may be the will be explained to you directly at interview).

3. The exact start time and schedule of the company. If the working time for the office staff fluctuates between certain hours, you will need to agree to a specific person of the exact date.

4. What a dress code is adopted in the company.

5. Do you need to bring documents on the first day, and if so, which ones. How the hiring documentation process will be organized.

6. You can specify what software you will need to use at work.

Treat the information and write it down in a notebook, PDA or mobile phone. It is best to immediately find for yourself a tool to fix the information that you will use during the trial period.

In some companies, it is assumed that your head briefly introduces you to your colleagues to get acquainted with them, somewhere it all depends on you. Do not hesitate to ask the question in advance HR-manager or supervisor at the signing of a job offer - it will help you prepare, plan your behavior.

Also, do not neglect the opportunity to write about yourself in the internal corporate blog / forum, if it is accepted in a company or department.

CONCLUSION

In today job market, it is not enough to have an outstanding resume and valuable skills, it is important to be a good marketer to be able to sell yourself. Any interview - it's like negotiating the sale. Therefore, it makes sense to approach its passage as business negotiations: first collect information as accurately as possible to identify needs and offer exactly what the client (in your case - employer) needs. The same goes for a job: the most important thing here is not the ability to nicely tell about yourself or embellish some of your skills. The main thing is to understand what from your vast experience can be interesting to the employer, and tell namely that.

During the interview, the employer seeks to learn more about your work activity, in particular, to find out your skills and experience, to assess whether you are able to adapt to work in the team and the organization as a whole. Remember that it is also an opportunity for you to learn more about your new role in the company, get more information about it and to draw conclusions about how the new position meets your plans for building a career in the future.

Preparing for the interview takes time. Careful planning and consideration of process of answering questions may take a week or more, depending on the importance of the upcoming interview. Training will allow you to prepare guaranteedly for an interview, and you will be able to present with benefit your knowledge, skills, abilities and skills necessary for work to which you are applying.

www.ingramcontent.com/pod-product-compliance
Lightning Source LLC
Chambersburg PA
CBHW061207180526
45170CB00002B/999